BEHIND EVERY SMILE

BEHIND EVERY SMILE

**Pictures, poems and thoughts
inspired by experiences of working with street children**

Ashley Coggins

Authentic

MILTON KEYNES ● COLORADO SPRINGS ● HYDERABAD

First published 2008 by Authentic Media
9 Holdom Avenue, Bletchley, Milton Keynes, Bucks, MK1 1QR, UK
1820 Jet Stream Drive, Colorado Springs, CO 80921, USA
Medchal Road, Jeedimetla Village, Secunderabad 500 055, A.P., India
www.authenticmedia.co.uk

Authentic Media is a division of IBS-STL U.K., limited by guarantee, with its
Registered Office at Kingstown Broadway, Carlisle, Cumbria, CA3 0HA.
Registered in England & Wales No. 1216232. Registered charity 270162

British Library Cataloguing in Publication Data
A catalogue record for this book is available from the British Library

ISBN-13: 978-1-86024-721-7

Cover Design by four-nine-zero design.
Page design by Temple design
Print Management by Adare
Printed and bound in Great Britain by Bell & Bain Ltd., Glasgow

Dedication

This book is dedicated to all the street children in the world today. I hope and pray that as their lives unfold, conditions will improve for them and they will be given opportunities to make something of their lives.

Contents

Acknowledgements

I would like to acknowledge the following people in the writing of this book. Firstly, the children and adults who live in poverty and who have inspired my writings. Also, my wife, Chris: thank you for sharing my journey, always believing in me, and for your unfailing love and support; Gill Bowker, a great friend, for your encouragement and enthusiasm for this project: your advice has been invaluable; Malcolm Down and the team at Authentic, for your faith in venturing into new territory. And lastly, thank you to you, the reader.

Foreword

I think my English teacher would laugh in disbelief if he knew I'd had a book published. He'd fall on the floor in hysterics if told it included poetry!

Writing has always been very personal for me, so it is not easy or natural to share my inner thoughts with other people. This book has only come about because my wife mentioned to a dear friend that I wrote poetry. From her response was born the vision of benefiting the very children who had inspired my writing.

I hope you enjoy reading the poems, written while working with street children. I apologise if some seem a little raw but they were often written as the event was actually happening – it's a bit like live television, not always as polished as it could be. I hope that as you read the background to each poem you will be 'in the moment' with me, captured in time, living the experiences and feeling the emotions as if witnessing them for yourself.

This is not a book about sadness, although I must admit there is sadness amongst the pages – it is a book of hope. Hope for the millions of street children in the world today.

Ashley Coggins

IT'S JUST ANOTHER DAY

This poem is based on my everyday experience and the daily sights and people I have come to notice as I cycle along streets where my wife and I work. Their lives change so little but each day they are able to motivate themselves. People can be so resilient in the most extreme situations and I have nothing but admiration for them.

It's Just Another Day

It's just another day! I see the blind man on the street
Walking in the gutter with his stick to guide his feet.
The world seems to ignore him, each one just passes by,
Blind man in his poverty, but it's us who have no eyes.

It's just another day! I pass the man who has no legs,
Selling lottery tickets when he could just sit and beg.
He moves himself along with his knuckles on the road –
A man who knows for sure, these streets aren't paved with gold.

It's just another day! I see the man with just one arm,
Balancing on his cycle, it causes great alarm.
Trying to sell his wares to anyone who'll buy,
He seems to sell so little but every day he tries.

It's just another day! I pass the boy who's selling gum,
He ought to be in school and having lots of fun.
When you live in poverty, life can be really cruel
But it would take so little to put this boy through school.

It's just another day! I see the rubbish picker in the bin,
With holes in her clothes, looking painfully thin;
The stench from the bin, makes me turn away,
But the rubbish she collects will buy her food today.

I look and I think, could I walk in their shoes
If every single day there was no other path to choose?
I guess I'd just accept it and struggle to make my way;
But would I have the motivation for just another day?

A LIFE WITHOUT LOVE

There are many children who have to live in an uncaring world. Street children have many things to contend with in their daily struggle for survival. Finding food and shelter is hard, but the one thing some of them may never experience in their lives is finding love in any form. That is so sad.

A Life Without Love

A young girl alone; she lives on the street.
Dressed in rags, no shoes on her feet.
Each day she sits, begging something to eat;
No home, no bed, the kerb is her seat.

Holds out her hand, the dirt's like a glove;
It's hard to keep clean without a bathtub!
Her life is so hard living down in the mud,
But the hardest of all is her life without love.

ANGELS WITH DIRTY FACES

I meet with many children, often living in dire situations. Many of them have developed character and personality traits that in the UK we would associate with criminality. Boys who are sly and dishonest; girls who have developed a hardness to protect themselves from their circumstances.

After many years of working and interacting with these children and young people, I have learnt that there is a lot of good inside them. 'Angels with Dirty Faces' sums that up. They may be scruffy and dirty and possibly wild, but inside every rogue there is good – sometimes you just have to look a little deeper!

Angels with Dirty Faces

These are the angels with dirty faces
The children who live in dark, dark, places.

Boys with scheming and slyness in the eye,
Girls who are tough and who no longer cry.

These are the children who many think are wild
But when you get to know them, inside is just a child.

Theirs is a life that's so hard to perceive . . .
Thrown out like rubbish that nobody needs.

Abandoned, unwanted, they are the world's shame
But God knows these children and carries their pain.

These are the angels with dirty faces;
In the kingdom of heaven they'll have special places.

LA LA

We all know people who keep smiling through, no matter what, and are an inspiration to those around them. La La is one of those people. Whatever life throws at her, she always smiles. She is also a support to her peers and, for someone so young, an inspiration to all who meet her.

La La

La La, La La, it sounds like a song
The name of a street girl who skips along;
Always she greets us with a big grin
Working the streets as each day begins.
Following tourists who might buy her swag –
The odd little trinket, a band or a bag.
She's never 'pushy', quite matter-of-fact
But from her task nothing ever distracts.
Ten years old, working twelve hours a day
Sent by her parents struggling on poor pay.
Out in all weathers, seven days a week,
If she wasn't so cheerful, her life would be bleak.
Her smile so infectious, her name like a rhyme,
A bright ray from heaven on earth to shine.

CHILDREN OF THE DUST

Nicknamed 'the children of the dust', there are many children living on the rubbish tips of the world. They scavenge in the rubbish to find items that can be recycled to buy food. The tips smell, the children smell and they are the outcasts of society, the lowest of the low.

Children of the Dust

Children of the dust; scratching for their daily crust
In the filth and squalor. No dreams for their tomorrow!

Children of the dust; no one that they can trust.
Open to exploitation. What a wretched situation.

Children of the dust; looked on with disgust,
They have no illusion; their life one of exclusion.

Children of the dust; the shame of all of us!
On the rubbish tips they dwell, innocents, exposed to hell.

DIFFERING VIEWS

Many of the places where street children and poor people head is for the tourist beach areas. This is because tourists are seen as a way to make money. Unfortunately, especially with more and more all-inclusive resorts, very little goes into the local economy. In fact, some resorts give the impression that the locals are something to be feared, and occasionally, often through desperation, incidents can happen.

On one side, there's how the tourist perceives the place they're visiting. Often at the end of their two-week break they dream of staying, living in the paradise they are reluctant to leave behind. Then there is the local view. People struggling to feed their families see more and more hotels becoming all-inclusive. Less and less money goes into the local economy. The locals think all tourists are extremely wealthy; from their point of view, they would need a king's ransom to stay one week in a hotel. They also get a bit agitated that people come to their country and do not want to spend any money or meet local people. The first thing many would do, if they were able, is get on the plane with the tourist and fly to where they believe paradise is.

Differing Views

Holidays, holidays, they can be such fun;
Lazy days spent on a lounger in the sun.
Blue sky, blue sea, this is paradise,
All of the locals seem really nice!
A beach hotel that towers in the sky –
It's all inclusive so I don't have to buy.
Secure in the complex, it's all so unique,
I live like a king for my precious two weeks.
The locals, they're so lucky. 'Tis paradise for sure.
O how I'd love to stay, have that shack upon the shore.

Working, working, all of the day;
If I sell no goods, I don't get pay.
Blue sky, blue sea, it's hard in the sun.
If tourists don't buy, no food for my son.
We live in the shack by the beach hotel,
No toilet, no water, not paradise but hell.
The tourists in their palace, live in a cocoon.
The whole of my shack could fit in their bathroom.
They're tourists, so lucky, they've never been poor,
They've never had to live in a shack upon the shore.

CHRIS (TINE)

In Asia the children find it difficult to pronounce 'Ch' so my wife's name, Christine, is difficult to say; hence, the children affectionately call her 'Tine'.

This is a poem about a wonderful human being. Working with the poor was always my dream and Chris has taken to it like a 'duck to water'. She puts everyone at ease with her warm, friendly manner. A natural giver, children, especially street children, are drawn to her unconditional love.

Chris (Tine)

A poem for Chrissy, my dear little wife.
So much joy you bring to everyone's life
As you pass through this world on your spiritual way
Touching many lives with what you do and say.
Friend to the rich and servant of the poor.
To the children abandoned, a friend for sure.
One day you'll be surrendered to God above
And the legacy you'll leave will be one of endless love.

JAYNE

It was New Year's Eve and, for the third year, we were celebrating it in a foreign land. The night was hot, humid and starry. We were with 140 street children and we would not have wanted to be anywhere else in the world. Some of the children were a little upset and so Chris and I were spending time with them. I was sitting looking up at the stars with some of the children, when a young girl whose nickname was Jayne came and sat beside me. She started to cry. I asked her, 'What's the matter?' and she replied that she could not remember what her mother and father looked like any more. All she knew was that they didn't want her. I put my arm around her to comfort her and we stared out into infinity. I said a little prayer and a look of calm came over her. We just sat there together and, to the accompaniment of crickets clicking in the darkness, we gazed at the stars. A night that will live with me forever!

Jayne

Looking out into empty space
Wondering why I am in this place . . .
Jayne a street child held in my arms
A child so sad yet full of charms.
Taunted, tormented by her past
Memories hidden behind a mask.

Tonight her pain comes flooding out
I hold her close, reassure her doubt.
All I can offer, unconditional love
And the prayer I'm saying to God above.
As we both look out into timeless space
A look of contentment spreads over her face.

IMAGINE . . .

When Chris and I see children in difficult circumstances we always try to help. Sometimes it's more straightforward than others. But every time poverty confronts us, the thing we find ourselves pondering is the strength of character of those in the desperate situations, and their motivation to continue each day. 'Imagine' is a poem to make us think how we would cope in these terrible situations; but it takes it one stage further, in that we have to imagine as a child.

Imagine . . .

Let me take you on a journey of self-realisation . . .
Imagine yourself in a street child's situation.
Your start to the day is always the same,
You rise from your bed, in the rubbish, by the drain.

No shower to clean, the river's your bath;
Personal hygiene's a thing of the past.
Time now to scavenge for food for the day,
It's hunger that drives you, you've no time to play.

Your family becomes other kids on the street;
They teach you your morals, you learn how to cheat.
Of course there are dangers you encounter too,
Dodging the pimps who would prostitute you.

Begging in the darkness, most ignore your plight;
Tiredness overcomes you in the middle of the night.
Hungry and tired you lay down by your drain,
Knowing tomorrow will be more of the same.

HYENAS OF THE STREET

Chris and I were cycling home one night from one of the street children's homes. We pulled our bikes over to a local market stall to get some fruit. I was sitting on my bike watching the world go on around me. Out of the darkness came two children, aged about seven. The atmosphere began to change as they dodged in and out of the bikes and people. They started picking up the squashed fruit on the road and eating it. Then five bigger boys, aged between nine and thirteen, appeared. At this point it reminded me of the African wildlife documentaries one sees. It was as if the younger boys were the tracker hyenas sent out to find food, and when they found it, the pack would arrive. The boys were all looking for 'food opportunities' and all the people were watching their bags!

Chris bought some extra fruit and took it over to the boys. The stallholder watched her do this and then he also gave the children some fruit. Like a pack, they then dispersed into the darkness and the area became calm again as they disappeared into the night.

Hyenas of the Street

Like a whirlwind they appear, the hyenas of the street!
When you're least expecting them, out of the darkness they creep.
Working as a pack, in their effort to survive
They know each trick in the book, as they run and duck and dive.
An opportunity presents itself, they surely will oblige!
The innocent and naive fall prey to the streetwise.

These children, some as young as five, live their lives in the dust,
Scavenging and working the streets to get their daily crust.
A world that does not love them, and teaches only hate
The only morals they know are the ones that they create.
Then as quick as they appeared, the pack goes out of sight
The hyenas of the street vanish into the night.

INNER LIGHT

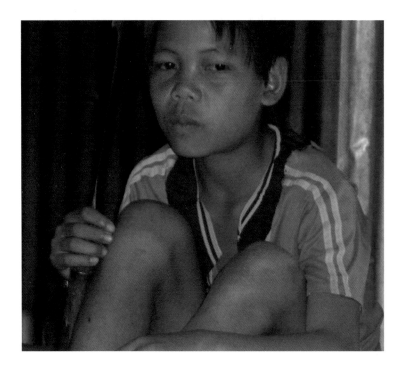

This poem is about a young boy who had spent his life on the streets and, although he had come into the street home, years of sniffing glue had affected his mental abilities. Everyone just left him to do his own thing because they said he was mad. We had experienced many children who had been glue-sniffers and, unlike in the UK where glue-sniffing is a recreational activity, street children tend to start sniffing glue to curb the hunger pangs.

Chris and I felt we could help him to learn. This was a boy who had never sat still in his life. He had no pencil skills and found it hard to concentrate. It was not a short process but we started to get results. The staff we worked with couldn't believe it. They started to see his inner light shine and said to us they would always look deeper in future!

Inner Light

He was a boy they all thought was mad,
But if you knew his life it was really sad.
A dustbin dweller, spent his life on the street,
Years of glue-sniffing, he had a sly streak!
The glue he had sniffed had damaged his brain,
But we could see deeper, he wasn't insane.
Eleven years old, never yet been to school,
So we started to teach him. They thought we were fools!
We set up a system to get him to learn,
The system worked well, new knowledge he yearned.
All were shocked except for us two,
The staff kept saying 'We hadn't a clue.'
But inside each person, there is a key
To help them develop, find their own destiny.
He'll not be a genius, we know that for sure,
But inside was something others chose to ignore.
The moral is this, if you give a child time
They'll find inner light, and learn how to shine.

A THOUSAND FLIES

I have decided that the best way of dealing with difficult situations is to create humour around them. Some mealtimes shared with the children are literally a fight with flies – sometimes you win, sometimes you lose. After many years of working and eating with street children, I seem to be getting over all my fussy ways!

A Thousand Flies

For people back in England this could be a bitter pill;
As we sit down with the children for the evening meal,
We can't see what we're eating because of all the flies!
That's why every meal we eat is such a big surprise!
A thousand flies enjoying what we're about to eat,
We're grateful for our chopsticks to fight them off the meat.
We then get really cocky and duel them for the rice,
But we're outnumbered for the fish – shame, it was so nice!
It's funny, as a child I was such a fussy kid,
But working with street children it's the normal way to live.

RUNAWAY MUM

I have many happy memories of Nee – watching her play 'jacks' with twigs and stones; her laughter as she tried to teach us local songs; Chris helping to wash her hair in the very cold river, and then getting rid of the nits . . . But I also have memories of her frustration boiling over, and temper tantrums – anger being vented due to being abandoned by her mother. Like so many of the children we come across, her father was missing and her mother had found a new man and gone off with him. When we face these situations here in the UK, we have financial assistance and social services. In the places where we work there are no such luxuries; the children usually end up on the streets trying to support themselves.

Runaway Mum

Nee's the child of a runaway mum,
At eight years old, it's not much fun.
Her mother's gone off with her new man.
Not easy for Nee to understand.
Now living her life with all the strays,
Selling her trinkets for food each day.

Poor little Nee carries a heavy weight,
Her little mind's full of anger and hate.
Filled with rejection, it sometimes spills out,
And when it does, at the tourists she shouts!
Such a heavy burden for one so young,
She's one of many, rejected by her mum.

THE POVERTY CYCLE

The best way out of the poverty cycle is to learn a trade. If the younger generation can be taught skills for jobs where there are shortages, then the children have a better chance of being able to support themselves financially . . . and this will benefit the country's economy.

In many developing and Third World countries, education is not free so the poor cannot send their children to school. The children have no skills. Employers keep the wages low and profits high and, of course, there's no benefit system. So it's work for a small wage – or starve!

These young lads are being given the chance to learn skills so they can break the cycle of poverty. We are supporting them through a two-year vocational training course in motorcycle repairs.

The Poverty Cycle

Poverty gets on its cycle and rides round the world,
Turning out beggars in the shape of boys and girls,
Down the generations from father to son –
The wheels keep turning as poverty rides on.
Poverty is a cycle, without a chain or gears,
But it keeps on going for year after year.
How do we stop it, they say it can't be done;
So the rich man keeps on pedalling, and the poor man has to run.
The cycle must be broken so where do we begin?
The answer – education, vocational trade training.
Teach the poor a trade and help them find a job;
Break the poverty cycle, no poor to oil the cog.
When the cog stops turning, the wheels will stop for sure,
And the cycle of poverty? Broken for ever more.

BABIES FOR SALE

There have been many stories in the news of couples who have adopted a child only to find out that the child was not an orphan. The parents, living in extreme poverty, had been convinced by an intermediary that their child would have a better life in the West, and they were given a small amount of money.

Although we have not witnessed this in our work, 'Babies for Sale' was my response to a television documentary, detailing the facts and highlighting the challenging situation that exists.

There are many orphanages in Asia doing a wonderful job, but it's sad that there is a darker side to this valuable work.

Babies for Sale

Babies for adoption! Couples come from the West
Keen to care for a baby, relieve its distress.
Poor little orphans, all alone in the world,
There are so many babies, boys and girls.
But the truth may not be all that it seems,
As desperate couples fulfil their dreams.

Abandoned, unwanted, just sold for a price.
Who can resist this bundle so nice?
Sad to say the truth is a lot less clear!
This child, thought an orphan, has parents so dear.
Sometimes these babies have parents for sure
But they give them up because they're so poor.

They'll sell their child for just one month's money.
They now eat bread, but the 'brokers' eat honey.
The brokers and middlemen, they have it made.
Babies? Big business! A nice little trade!
When people are poor you just name your price.
The cost of a baby? Just one sack of rice.

ICE CREAM

Chris and I were in an area bordering China and it was freezing cold. I was drawn to this little girl, who was smiling while eating an ice cream. We struck up a conversation and she told me her parents were opium addicts and she is sent out to work on the streets selling trinkets to tourists to support their habit. This particular day she had sneaked some of the money and treated herself to an ice cream. Unfortunately, there are some children whom it is difficult to help. This girl had parents, even though they were trading on her childhood, and we were just a couple of foreigners. Sometimes, hard as it is, we just have to accept that there is very little we can do.

Ice Cream

There she sat eating an ice cream,
Her story I could never have dreamed.
Her eyes were sad but she wore a smile,
So I stopped to talk to her for a while.
Just a child only eight years old,
But working hard on the streets so cold.
Twelve hours a day without a break,
Each penny she earned her mother would take.
Her parents were addicts of the poppy seed
And the money she made satisfied their need.
I wished that opium was out of her life
And that fun and happiness could replace the strife.
We smiled at each other. She went on her way,
But somewhere she's out there, twelve hours a day.

YEN

When I first met Yen he seemed a pretty unruly and angry lad, but then, if we had been in his shoes, I'm sure most of us would have been the same.

Six months later he was a totally different boy, like so many we were helping. I have singled him out because underneath his angry face there was a wonderful infectious smile. He was just one of many success stories. It's marvellous to see how just being there for these children who come from the streets, and giving them time, really can help them decide to turn their lives around.

Yen

He was an angry-faced boy when first I met him,
But he left his mark. I will never forget him,
A boy of twelve made hard by the street.
He was one of many, he wasn't unique.
We taught him to play, he learned to share,
And as time went on he learned to care.
Behind the toughness was hidden a child,
After six months he was no longer wild.
We took him and clothed him, he looked pretty cool!
With lots of encouragement he was ready for school.
Our work was now done, time to move on
To find more children who've done no wrong.
We leave very quietly never making a fuss,
Never knowing where next our journey will lead us.
I'll always remember Yen's wave goodbye,
If he'd known we were leaving, I knew he would cry;
I just turned and smiled; he'd become a young man,
But there are others who need us. I hope he understands.

SNIFF SNIFF SNIFF

As I mentioned in the introduction to 'Inner Light', many street children sniff glue to curb hunger pangs; they also do it to keep warm. This poem is about the children I have come to know who had been glue-sniffers, but in particular, a beautiful young girl called Rae whose little arms were badly scarred from self-abuse.

I'll always remember Rae and the first time I saw what she had done to her arms. I love to make children laugh and Rae was no exception. She had such a beautiful smile, but hidden behind that smile was her sad past life. And hidden behind my smile were the tears in my heart for her.

Sniff Sniff Sniff

Sniff sniff sniff, that eases the pain.
Another day, no food again.
Get me high, take me out of hell.
Hunger disappears with the fumes I smell.

Sniff sniff sniff, my life's no use,
Cuts on my arms from self-abuse.
Parents abandoned me, went away.
At ten years old I'm a kid who's a stray.

Sniff sniff sniff, no pain any more.
I can't understand what I'm living for.
What's the purpose of being alive?
As day to day I struggle to survive.

Sniff sniff sniff, I'm as high as a kite.
It's not the answer, won't make things right!
As the glue wears off I feel really sick,
If I had some food this habit I'd kick.

DAY OF THE NITS

Wherever we have worked with street children there have
been plagues of nits, and Vietnam is no exception. Chris had
discovered that some new children who had come into one
of the street homes had not come alone! Their heads were
alive with head lice which had quickly spread to all the other
children. She took control of the situation and organised
mass showers and hair-washing. I joked with her that at
school she would have been the nit nurse! She ended up de-
nitting 120 street children, all the staff and ourselves.
Everyone then received their own personal nit comb for
future use!

Day of the Nits

Nits were rife in the street children's homes!
It's not easy to leave your head alone.
You feel an itch and then one or two more –
It's time to de-louse children's homes, one to four.
Call in the nit nurse! She doesn't exist.
So in Vietnam we call out for Chris.
'Chris the nit nurse' made everyone laugh!
The children were made to shower and bath.
A million nits later, the job's finally done . . .
But we'll do it again if she misses just one!

BEHIND EVERY SMILE

Behind all the smiles of street children I have come to know there are stories that reach deep into your heart . . .

Behind Every Smile

A joyful smile spread across a young face,
A sign of happiness, never out of place.
Yet in their eyes I glimpse stories so sad
Of the life they once lived and the trauma they had.

There's the street boy who threw himself off the bridge
Because he no longer had the will to live.
Thankfully spotted and brought to a home,
A new chance in life, no longer alone.

A young girl of nine, parents died on the street;
Each night in the market in rubbish she'd sleep.
She is found and brought to a street children's home;
For once in her life she's a bed of her own.

These children still keep all their pain in their soul
And wear a big smile so no one will know.
Next time you see a smile so wide,
Try looking behind to the story it hides.

CHILDREN OF 'NO MAN'S LAND'

This poem is about an absolutely fascinating border crossing – there is so much cultural challenge as 'modern' Thailand meets the poverty of Cambodia; cars and wooden barrows meet. You see poor Cambodian people pulling these wooden carts with all their worldly possessions and families in them. Then you are struck by all the children running around in the 'No Man's Land' area, begging from the tourists and locals. These children do not have passports or papers; they have nowhere to keep them, and their 'home' is the border area where they are guaranteed food.

Children of 'No Man's Land'

Remember the story of Peter Pan
The boy who lived in Never-Never Land?

I'll tell you a story, it's about children too,
In a land called 'No Man's', sadly it's true.

The place where they live is a faraway land,
A border between Cambodia and Thailand.

Unlike Peter Pan who never grew up,
Their childhood is lost; so young, so corrupt.

They have no families, no bed, no home,
Children so young, left to fend on their own.

Making a living from what they can beg,
Folk at the border see that they're fed.

Young boys and young girls, some look so sweet
It's hard to believe they live on the street.

If you've been to this border, then you'll understand,
There's no happy ending in 'NO MAN'S LAND'.

TOURIST SEX SLAVES

In Asia, young girls are sometimes tricked into the sex trade. They are taken from their villages on the pretence that they will be given a good job so they can send money home to help support their poor families. Unfortunately, they are then forced into prostitution to pay back money that was given to their parents. The parents are usually oblivious to this and think their daughters have work in factories.

The reality is they are imprisoned and used as sex slaves for the tourists and locals, often only released when they are infected with HIV. Unless it can be stopped, girls like these in the photo may one day become prey to this evil trade.

Tourist Sex Slaves

Girls young and sweet,
Ripe tourist meat.
They have no voice,
They have no choice.
Twenty men a day!
The mob takes the pay.
A death sentence ahead
From each man in bed.
The future is Aids,
For these young sex slaves.

REFLECTION

In our early days of doing this work, friends very kindly helped us raise enough money to buy new clothes for 150 children (who were very shoddily dressed) living in a street children's home. We took the money back with us and arranged to take small groups of children out so that for the first time in their lives they could choose their own clothes. This was one of those memorable experiences in life that you never forget, and feel so privileged to have shared. There are so many stories to tell of taking these children into a store! They never dreamed they would be allowed to enter it, let alone be able to buy clothes. This poem literally reflects one of those 'take your breath away' experiences.

I was with a lad named Eck who was eight years old. We were looking for clothes when all of a sudden he gave a shriek and ran behind me. I looked to see what the problem was, but all I could see in front was a full-length mirror reflecting my image, and Eck peering around from behind me. Initially he had a concerned expression on his face; then it became inquisitive. He stepped out and began to look at himself in the mirror. He pulled some faces, wobbled his body a little and then started smiling at himself, as if he had accepted his reflection. What I came to realise was that he had never seen himself full-length before and was obviously shocked at how he looked in the rags he was wearing. He then began his shopping with extreme enthusiasm, and was very grateful to be able to buy new clothes so he could look like other children in the store.

Reflection

Illusion
Confusion
Seeing yourself at last
Reflection
Imperfection
Poverty unmasked

Knowing
Showing
Who you really are
Connecting
Accepting
Image in the glass

ENGLISH LESSON

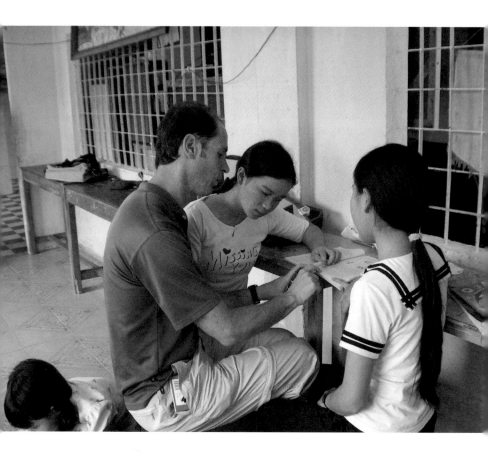

For many years I have been helping children in street homes with English pronunciation. In Asia, grammar is not really a problem for them; in fact, many have a better understanding of it than I do!

However, they tend to have problems pronouncing their Rs and Ls, often switching the sounds around. This can be difficult to understand at first but once you get to grips with the problem, it can be quite amusing. They also have a pronunciation problem with one or two other sounds, and maybe one day I'll write a poem about those. Who knows!

English Lesson

Here's a little riddle. I really must confess
Until I got my head round it, it caused me much distress.
Teaching street children English, they have a problem with two sounds.
The *Rs* and the *Ls*, they always switch them around.
One night for my dinner, they said we had *'flied lice'*;
I just smiled very politely and said – that sounds really nice!

Reading from their book, they say 'He's lost his *loof'*,
And the *'lains'* coming in; there, you can see the *'ploof'*.
Or they would read about *'Lodger'* whose dog has *'lun'* away.
I have to start thinking *'raterarry'* to understand what they say!

Try a little *'plactice'* you don't have to change much,
'Ploblems' with your gears, that'll be your *'crutch'*.
If you're *'vely rucky'*, you get it straight away,
It makes it so much easier to work out what they say.
To the unprepared, it leaves them all confused,
But for me, their English teacher, it keeps me quite amused!

SHOESHINE

Shoeshine boys are a common sight in Asia. They make a living from local trade but their goal is to 'strike it lucky' and persuade a tourist to have their shoes polished. For them, this is the perfect opportunity to make a whole day's wage in just one job. They will charge a 'tourist' price, and then sometimes sneakily push this up – as a friend of mine experienced. When his shoes were given back to him, the price had doubled! He started to debate this with the lad who insisted he had done a small repair as well. My friend's travelling companion laughed, pointing out to him that he was arguing over pennies, but he said it was the principle! Technically he was right, but sometimes we have to relax our principles. If we had to live the shoeshine lad's life, then we'd understand more about hunger and the fear of not knowing where the next meal is coming from. So I would say: If this happens to you, swallow your pride, smile and think, 'I've done my bit for charity today.'

Shoeshine

'Shoeshine, shoeshine, only one dollar!'
As they chase the tourist that's what they holler.

These are young boys who don't go to school,
But they're really sharp, they're nobody's fool.

They play on your conscience and push up the price.
To you it's just pennies, to them, extra rice.

So if you're caught out, just smile inside.
Their art of survival? Taking you for a ride!

THIS IS THE HAND

This is the hand that once had to beg,
Depending on others for its daily bread.
Now it learns with machines to sew;
Learning a trade is the way to go.

This is the hand that picked through the bins,
Surviving each day from rubbish recycling;
Now this hand cuts and washes the hair,
A chance of a trade after a life of despair.

The hand of a pickpocket caused people to dread,
Now learning to repair motorcycles instead . . .
A life, once survived by turning to crime,
Now given a chance to leave poverty behind.

The hand that pulls the embroidery needle,
Once starving and cold, a body so feeble,
Now making pictures of beautiful art,
A life once so dark, given a new start.

The hand of poverty learning a trade,
Vocational training, another life saved.
All these hands now have a new way,
And we're reaching out to more each day.

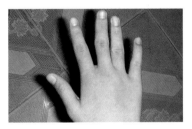

The beauty that these hands now produce,
Hides bitterness past and their previous use.

**Were it not for the opportunity to receive
vocational training, these hands would have continued
on their original course and in their life of poverty.**

PIED PIPER

This poem was written after events covering a few days and nights when we would take small groups of poor children to get blankets and shoes. Events that brought absolute joy to them and us! These were children who spent their lives working on the streets selling trinkets. They would skip, dance, sing and giggle as they followed us through the streets to get items to bring warmth into their difficult lives. Hearing them giggling and skipping along behind us, it reminded me of the Pied Piper of Hamlyn.

Pied Piper

Children shuffling along the street,
No shoes, little clothing, not much to eat.
Heads held high in the freezing cold.
Many of these children may never grow old.

Children aware there's a change on the street,
Two people who care for them, quite unique.
Like the Pied Piper playing a tune,
The children dance, forgetting their gloom.

Children dancing along the street;
Children who've never had shoes on their feet;
Skipping, running, no more blues
Children so happy. They now have shoes.

Children giggling along the street,
Holding blankets to warm them when they sleep.
All of their lives they have frozen at night,
This little token brings such delight.

Children world over whose life is the street,
Wouldn't it be great if their lives were complete?
A world that cared, where each child had a chance
To follow the Piper and giggle and dance.

RUBBISH TIP

We had been working with a group of street children and had come to realise that many of them did have parents, but sadly they were so poor they could not afford to feed them. Chris and I always carried food and water with us to give to the many rubbish pickers we encountered on the streets. We decided to take this one stage further. We started taking food onto the nearby rubbish tips where we knew there was hunger. Our aim was to try to keep these families together, and prevent the children breaking away and ending up on the streets where they would be exposed to exploitation and danger.

I will always remember the first rubbish tip we visited. We took food to families with young children and babies living in desperate conditions amongst the stench of rotting waste, rats and snakes.

Rubbish Tip

It's hard to know where I can begin
To explain these thoughts I have within.
Just having worked on my first rubbish tip –
A family so poor with a father who's sick.
No food to eat, not for many a day –
You don't get food without money to pay.
A home, made of poles and a polythene sheet,
Stiflingly hot in this tropical heat.
They say 'count your blessings'; I sure did that day.
I was the lucky one. I could walk away.

CHILDREN OF THE SEWER

A television documentary uncovered the fact that in many countries street children are seen as vermin because, for many, crime follows them. To survive they steal. Many have never had the benefit of good role models to teach them right from wrong. So, groups of vigilantes hunt them down on the streets to kill them. There is usually not much incentive to stop these groups because many believe they are removing the criminals.

So, at night, many children who live on the streets where this happens go down into the sewer drains to sleep safely. In some countries babies have been born in these drains to street children, and so the cycle of poverty continues into the next generation. While we have not seen this ourselves in Asia, the plight of such children, made so clear in the programme, prompted me to write this poem.

Children of the Sewer

In the silver moonlight, you see their silhouette
As they scurry in the darkness, not into safety yet.
Scared of their shadow, should it give them away
These, the sewer children, who are only safe by day.

As the sun starts setting, the death squads will appear
Their twisted objective, to make street kids disappear.
With guns cocked and loaded, they look for kids to kill
Like a fantasy movie, it seems rather surreal.

Death squads on the streets play their deadly game.
The children's only safety is to hide in sewer drains.
Treated like vermin they don't have any rights
So beneath the city pavements they retreat every night.

Who can blame these children, drugs and sniffing glue
When hunger fills your tummy and despair's your future too.
So what of the future, for these kids who hide in drains?
Unless the world can stop it, it'll be more of the same.

ASHERLEEN

All my life, children have interpreted and pronounced my name in their own unique way. I remember two street children who were both saying my name wrongly, and arguing which one of them was right. They were shocked when I corrected them both.

This poem is about a young girl who was very independent. At seven years old she had been fending for herself on the streets and never gave any impression that she needed to connect with anyone. But for some reason she started asking for me every time she saw Chris. She would come looking for me – I was usually teaching some lads badminton or football – and she would call out: 'Asherleen!' I would never say that any one child is more special than any other . . . but some memories are more special than others.

Asherleen

'Asherleen!' O how I love to hear my name
From a beautiful street child, not out for gain.
She just wants to love me, and give me her affection
When I arrive at the project, she heads in my direction.
Through my hair she goes, looking for nits.
At every opportunity by my side she sits.
But one day soon I'll be gone far from here
I hope my leaving doesn't cause her a tear.
I expect I'll be forgotten just like a good dream
But me, I'll always remember how she called me 'Asherleen'.

JOURNEY OF THE STREET (1)

The problems with poverty are vast. It is estimated that there are more than 25 million street children living in Asia alone. Today, somewhere, there is a child starting the 'Journey of the Street', and we pray their young life will not end as the child in the poem.

However, there are two sides to every story, as you can see from the next poem, 'Journey of the Street (2)'. Chris and I are privileged to be able to work to help as many children as possible so they do not end up in the gutter, but are educated and trained.

Journey of the Street (1)

I'll take you on a journey, the journey of the street;
It tells you the story of how life can be so cheap.

A young boy abandoned, the street is now his home.
He stares – an addict dying in the gutter all alone.

The child that he was has now been lost.
Surrendered to the street, his childhood the cost.

At seven years old, finds his own food to eat,
Each and every night in the rubbish he'll sleep.

As the years go on his life looks bleak,
Day by day his life is the street.

Corruption, exploitation, he learns to play the game,
But others still exploit him for their own self gain!

As he grows older the spiral continues down,
Drugs drag him under and he begins to drown.

Dying in the gutter that has become his home,
In a world that didn't care, dying all alone.

Love has avoided him, and he's about to die.
No one to mourn him, no one to cry.

He gasps his last breath, from his body all life seeps . . .
A young boy stares down on him, and starts his journey
of the street . . .

JOURNEY OF THE STREET (2)

The young man in the picture above is one of many success stories. As a small boy he was fending for himself on the streets but thankfully, he was rescued and brought to a street children's home where he was given refuge and educated. After schooling, he did a vocational training course in hairdressing and now rents a very small unit which he shares with another lad. His life would have been so different if there had been no one to care. Like so many others undertaking the vocational training courses we support, his 'Journey of the Street', depicted in this poem, has a happy ending.

Journey of the Street (2)

I'll take you on a journey, the journey of the street;
It tells you the story of how we can help the weak.

A young boy abandoned, the street becomes his home.
He stares – an addict dying in the gutter all alone.

But if we work together, his childhood won't be lost.
Rescued from the street, £10 a month the cost.

Seven years old, at last a home and food to eat.
A street children's home, at last somewhere safe to sleep.

As the years go on his future's looking bright,
From his darker side of life, there is a shining light.

Allowed to be a child, he learns to play games,
In his life is happiness, where once was only pain.

As he grows older, he grows in self-esteem,
A future before him, living all his dreams.

In a world that showed it cared, for a boy once all alone,
Saved him from the streets, gave him a loving home . . .

Now he's loved and cherished, he's about to fly.
This would have been so different were none prepared to try.

Educated, trained, his future looks so neat . . .
At last we are breaking the journey of the street.

PRISONERS OF POVERTY

One night whilst watching life on the streets all around me, I became very aware of the freedom I have. Plane, train or bus, I have no restrictions; I can go anywhere I want in the world. The people in my poem have no such freedom – they are prisoners. Prisoners of poverty.

Prisoners of Poverty

Scraping a living from the street,
Unable to give your kids a treat.
Unsure what each day will bring,
No money, no food. Life's painful sting.

Little street children learning to steal,
Eating from dustbins. How does it feel?
No father to protect you in the night,
No one to love you, hold you tight.

Shoeshine boy shining the shoes;
This would not be the life you choose.
Struggling to survive each and every day,
Whether you eat depends on who will pay.

One day soon I will leave this place,
But in my mind I'll carry each face.
Me, I have choices, I can leave at any time,
While they serve their sentence – poverty their crime.

HANH

Imagine a tropical evening: the wind is warm, stars are bright in the sky, lighting the evening. I cycle past one of the schools in the area and hear a little voice. I look to see Hanh waving at me. I stop, thinking 'Wow, what is Hanh – a ten-year-old girl – doing out on the streets at this time of night?' She runs across to me and jumps on the cycle rack on the back of my bike. I start to cycle her to the street home, thinking if I had not been going past she would have had a long walk in darkness . . . Then I grin to myself for thinking in my Western way. For I remember that this is a girl, like so many others, who once had to fend for herself on the streets.

All of a sudden she squeezes me, her arms around my waist, and starts to giggle as she rests her head against my back. It's probably a long time – if ever – since she has had someone she could pretend is her dad. I cycle in the anarchy of the late-night traffic conscious of her little life in my hands.

Hanh

Little arms wrapped around my waist
As I cycle through this foreign place.
Little Hanh on my cycle rack,
Her happy face pushed close to my back.
Me a Westerner, from a different world,
She, a young Vietnamese street girl.
Pedalling in the darkness she sits there so proud.
Squeezing my waist she giggles out loud.
A child of the street no parents she had,
But tonight she pretends I'm her substitute dad!

ICY FINGERS

In some parts of Asia where Chris and I work, the temperatures can be as low as England in the winter. Many children are out on the streets, trying to earn a living from the tourists to help their families, back in their villages. They often have minimal amounts of clothing to keep them warm.

I remember the first time we went to a mountainous area bordering China. Like so many tourists, we went to see the beautiful scenery. However, within a few hours we realised how many poor, cold children there were on the streets. At night we would sit and talk with them. One time, a little girl put out her hands to hold mine. I said, 'Your hands are so cold.' She smiled and said, 'They are always cold.' I put them in my hands and started to warm them. The next day, we went to the market and brought lots of gloves. This was the start of many journeys to help these children.

Icy Fingers

Little fingers wrapped in mine
Together now our hands entwine.
Mine so warm in the freezing air,
Hers so cold, as this moment we share.

She smiles at me, it warms my heart
As I warm her fingers in the dark.
My heart goes out in admiration;
It's hard to survive in her situation!
A life in poverty is really rough.
When it's freezing cold, impossibly tough.

FLOWER CHILDREN

In Asia, many children are used to work on the streets to sell flowers. Often their biggest dream is to go to school but sadly, few get the chance, as they work day and night. They are usually well dressed but often hungry. When we see them, we give them food and make them laugh. Then at least we know they have been fed and had something to make them smile that day.

Flower Children

Flower children dodging the night-time traffic
In the stifling heat, their lives so tragic.
Cute little faces but legs badly scarred
Selling their flowers as they slip between cars.

If they sell their flowers they get food and a bed
But if they don't, they may be beaten instead.
Run by adults, some of whom are cruel,
Seldom a chance to go to school.

Posies and flower chains they look really nice –
But the money's taken from them, so please think twice.
If you see these children, give a meal not money
Then at least you'll know they have food in their tummy.

TAKE A LOOK IN THE MIRROR

Working with poverty has made me realise how fortunate I am to have been born in England! The saying is 'There but for the grace of God go I'. Most people's only contact with poverty is a glimpse on the news, which can be quite transient. When confronted face to face with the harsh reality, even the hardest heart would be moved. This mother and child were living in desperate conditions and, although we were able to help, the look in their eyes still haunts me.

Take a Look in the Mirror

Take a look in the mirror. What do you see?
Have you heard the expression 'face of poverty'?

Is this a face of a person you've seen?
Or just an expression of a face in a dream.

The 10 o'clock News gives us a small glimpse
And just for a moment we all start to wince.

A young father holding a dying son.
A child on the street who has no one.

Then in a flash the visions are gone . . .
Although they're still suffering, the news has moved on.

Yes poverty's not faceless; you can see it if you look
For some it is written, their face like a book.

I never feel easy when I stare in its face
Because there go we all but for God's good grace.

When you look in the mirror, what do you see?
Things could have been different, your face, poverty.

CLOTHES FROM ENGLAND

One summer when we were back in the UK, we asked all our friends if they had clothes their children had grown out of. Everyone was fantastic and the clothes came pouring in – we had all sizes. Chris then proceeded to sort them into 'boys' and 'girls' and different ages to make sure that when we returned to the street children's homes everyone would have something.

When we arrived back, we took all the clothes to the street children's homes and set them up: one side boys' clothes, the other side, girls'. It was a great experience watching these very excited young people sorting through the clothes and the amazing thing was everyone got something they wanted.

Clothes from England

Look at their faces; look at the joy!
Clothes from England for girls and for boys.
Each one has a chance to choose for themselves,
Don't care it was owned by somebody else.
Grateful for anything, it's a joy to receive
When you've lived on the street; it's like Christmas Eve.
The boys, they know, they instantly choose,
While the girls sift around through the pinks and blues.
Dithering and holding, they take so long,
While the boys have finished, got their new clothes on.
At last girls decide on their new clothes to wear
And it's smiles all around while brushing their hair.
At this point I turn to Chrissy, my girl,
At times like this, we've the best job in the world.

THE TREE OF GRIEF

This poem was written in memory of a sixteen-year-old girl who chose to eat the leaf of a poisonous tree because of her desperate poverty.

The poison is not instantaneous; it takes many hours to work. If the person who eats 'the leaf' tells someone within the first few hours, they are given the only antidote the locals know – dogs' excrement mixed in water which acts as an emetic. Unfortunately, this young girl never revealed this information, pretending she just had a headache and was tired. As time wore on, her boyfriend realised what she had done and frantically carried her down the mountain, a journey of many hours, heading for a very basic health clinic in town. Sadly, she didn't make it.

She was the older sister of a thirteen-year-old street girl called Shu, and just one of four victims of the 'Tree of Grief' that I was told about on my return to the area after a short spell back in England.

The Tree of Grief

Branches swaying in the breeze,
Gentle rhythm sighs through leaves.
Standing innocently, showing its splendour,
Beautiful flowers, elegant, slender.

No ordinary tree, a story to be told
Which, when you hear it, will make you go cold.
Locals will tell you they have the knowledge,
This, the tree with the deadly foliage.

There are those who eat its leaf;
Some so young, their lives so brief.
For them desperation is no novelty,
They eat 'the leaf' to escape their poverty.

Standing innocently showing its splendour
Beautiful flowers, elegant, slender.
Sways in the breeze, its poisonous leaf,
The sinister secret of the Tree of Grief.

EMOTIONAL ROLLER COASTER

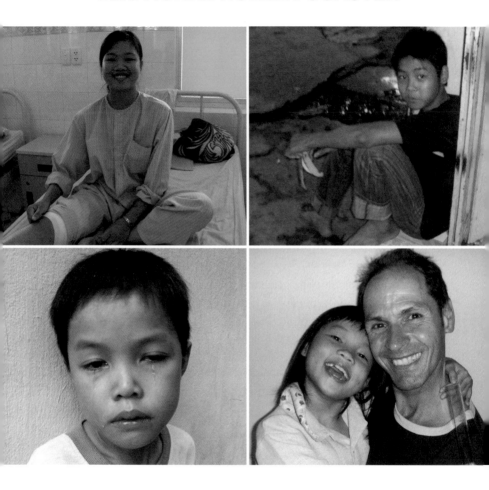

In our work there are times when our emotions are stretched to the limit in both directions, sometimes to the heights of pure joy, and sometimes to the deepest depths. I felt the best way to describe our life is – an emotional roller coaster: up, down, spinning around, adrenaline rushes and sickness in your stomach, sometimes all in a very short space of time. It is very much the ride of our life and, just like a roller coaster, it can be thrilling . . . also, quite scary. But our faith will always keep us holding on, right until the end of the ride.

Emotional Roller Coaster

No ordinary ride – it's the ride of your life
Sometimes we feel on the 'edge of a knife'!
Your emotions reach heights then dip right down low
With the challenges faced as we view life's show.

There isn't a G-force to help us get back!
We see hunger and sickness; it's hard not to crack.
All is so different from life in the West
For the unprepared – mind-blowing distress.

Emotions start tearing away at your heart
Seeing families scavenge for food in the dark.
It pulls, drags you down to feeling quite low;
The emotional coaster; round, round you go.

A heart operation, another life saved!
A young girl's been spared from an early grave.
Excited, delighted, the roller's on top –
Then hearts miss a beat as you see the drop!

The emotional coaster can be a hard ride
It teaches you who you have 'living inside'!
Adrenaline rushes, fear, dangers and trials
All part of the coaster's definitive style.

Romantic, exciting, some foolishly think;
But injustice and poverty make the heart sink.
There are the successes that make it worthwhile
But the emotional coaster has more tears than smiles.

RAK UNKNOWN

I have met many street children who have no idea when their birthday is. They do not even know their family name. When you live on the streets, the most important question every day is 'Where am I going to find a meal today?' so things like birth date/family name become irrelevant . . . and, because your family have abandoned you, they won't be calling around for your birthday.

Rak Unknown

His name was Rak Unknown.
He had no second name
He spent his life alone,
Carried his parents' shame.

He felt he had no worth.
His age he didn't know.
He had no date of birth,
No family, no home.

A beggar from the streets
But to us he's just a boy.
They say he lies and cheats
His character they destroy.

He's been misunderstood
He only needs a chance!
Give him shelter and some food
And he will change his stance.

THE LANGUAGE OF LOVE

Many people ask Chris and me how we communicate with the children we work with. 'Are you fluent in the language?' they ask. The truth is, in the last seven years we have lived in three different countries and our biggest problem when we start to learn a new language is that everyone wants to practise their English! So we tend only to pick up the basics. This usually astounds people; they say, 'How do you communicate, then?' Well, children – especially neglected children – respond to the universal language of the world, the language of love. We just show them we care, and make them laugh a lot.

The Language of Love

As we move from country to country, land to land
How do we make the street children understand?
Many different languages and tongues to speak
But ours is a language that's not really unique.
It does not need words or even a sound,
It's a language that's as simple as holding a hand.
A cuddle, a smile, or a great big hug,
All children understand the language of love.

THE LADY RUBBISH PICKER

Cycling late one night, I pulled my bike over to take in the beautiful warm night air. Out of the side of my eye, I caught sight of a young woman rummaging through the dustbins. She was quite pretty and it was obvious she could have chosen to make a living in a more immoral way. I was taken by her elegance as she rummaged through the dustbins. She looked across at me. As our eyes met – and she had beautiful eyes – it was as if our minds met as well. It was as if we were both working out what it must be like to live in each other's world.

Would I be able to move and live with such dignity, if I were in her shoes? It was a very humbling experience for me as I tried to imagine the prospect. Then, in the blink of an eye she was gone, probably to another bin. I looked around in the darkness but she was nowhere to be seen. Some people say you get hardened to poverty when you are around it all the time, but the truth is, you just don't show the emotions on the outside. The memory of that moment has stayed with me and comes back every time I read this poem.

The Lady Rubbish Picker

I stopped for a moment to take in the air
And in the darkness, a young woman stood there.

She was not proud, as she rummaged through the bins
Watching her do this, I felt humbled within.
Around her a city, with such wealth and greed
Yet she in her hardship, poverty and need.

She could have sold her soul, been a lady of the night
But walking the hard path, she chose to do right.
The journey she has is a hard path to tread
Gracefully she walks it, so her children can be fed.

She turned and our eyes met, for a moment in time
My heart went out to her, and so did my mind.
Our lives so different, but together in this place
Her soft eyes that looked, said much more than her face.

As quick as I saw her, she vanished in the dark
But the compassion I felt will remain in my heart.

THE PICTURE

There are so many sad young lives; children who we have met that have been through awful situations. This is a poem about one such boy, about fourteen years old, who had been exploited by adults, and how he came to trust two adults who were foreigners – because he knew we cared.

He was brought to the street home by the police who had caught him stealing. Rather than put him in a detention centre they felt he deserved a chance. Over the next couple of months we gained his trust and, for the first time in a long while, he was around adults who were not trying to take advantage of him in any way. Then, one day he came to us with a picture he had drawn. He tried to explain about the picture but we didn't quite understand. He then gave us a hug. We just smiled and put his picture away until later. The next day we were told he had run away. We got his picture out and looked much closer; the hills, a shack, two graves and a figure. We worked out that the two graves were his dead parents; the figure, his grandmother; the shack, her house. We assumed he was heading home over 500 miles north back to his grandmother. We prayed he made it safely.

The Picture

I remember a street boy; we may never meet again.
He had lived a life of horror, his name was Cheng.
They say that our eyes are the windows of our soul –
When first I met Cheng, his were empty, black holes.

His parents both dead, of his age he was unsure.
His grandma took him in, although she was poor.
No schooling for him, he had to beg each day
The money that he made just helped to pay his way.

Tricked by a bus driver, a free trip to the beach!
His village and grandmother, now far out of reach.
Sold into prostitution and chained in a cell.
A year before he could escape from that life of hell.

Brought to the street home where we did our work
We tried to heal his pain, his mistrust, guilt and hurt.
Then one day he came, with a picture he had drawn
The very next day he disappeared into the dawn.

We know now the picture was of his journey's end,
He was saying goodbye to his two English friends.

TEARS IN MY HEART

Injustice is a frequent travelling companion. Sometimes we are able to help; sadly, sometimes we are not. Often it is said to me, 'How do you do what you do without getting emotional?'

The truth is, I do feel emotional but I have learnt to keep my emotions inside me. Life has treated many of the children we work with harshly, but they rarely cry in self-pity. When their tears do overflow I am always there to support them – I have tears too, but mine are well out of view. They are inside my heart.

Tears in My Heart

How precious it is, the gift of a child.
Into this world, so gentle and mild,
But society moulds them, to good or to bad
Depending upon life experiences they've had.

We pray they have smiles, and lots of fun.
Worries and evil, we pray they have none.
But there are children, through no fault of their own,
Who live on the streets with no real home.

Exploited by adults, child labour is cheap,
Often no more than a dollar a week.
Then there are others, trapped in the sex trade,
Degraded, tormented, alone and afraid;
Each time I see them, injustice leaves its mark
And for each precious child, I cry tears in my heart.

THE LOTTERY OF LIFE

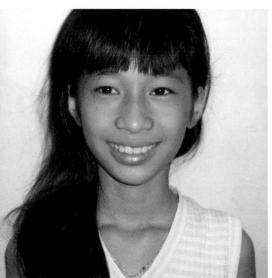

It was about 8 o'clock in the evening when I turned a corner and was confronted by a father and daughter sitting on the pavement outside a hotel, begging. The young girl looked sweet but very poor. A car pulled up and a girl about the same age got out with her parents. She was beautifully dressed. The poor girl just sat there staring, looking her up and down, while her father tried to beg from the parents. The parents took their daughter's hand and they all walked into the hotel, oblivious to the little girl and her father. The poor little girl's eyes followed them as they walked past; she was looking at the clothes and cleanliness of the rich girl. I felt I could almost read her thoughts. Maybe it was just my perception; maybe I was just meant to be in that place at that time. Sometimes it is not easy to be a spectator in the theatre of life. Unlike a play where the actors take off their costumes and enter their real lives again, for the poor girl and her father there was no changing their roles in the 'lottery of life'.

The Lottery of Life

It happened one night on the streets of Saigon
It was over in seconds, it didn't take long.
A young girl and her father, begging on the street
When out of a car came a family so chic
A girl the same age but beautifully clad
Holding the hands of her mum and dad.
The poor girl begging, stared into her face –
'If life had been different I could be in your place!'
The rich girl and family were quite unaware
Of the father and daughter who were begging just there.
Over in a moment, it did not last that long
But to the poor girl begging, it must have seemed so wrong;
The lottery of life sometimes pricks like a thorn . . .
It dictated for this girl the place she was born.

MR AND MRS HELLO

The fact that so many people shout 'Hello!' as we cycle past them in our daily work prompted me to write this. They all feel as if they know these two foreigners working in their country. I joke with Chris that they think we're called 'Mr and Mrs Hello'.

Mr and Mrs Hello

Hello! Hello!
A thousand times a day
As the only two foreigners
We stand out on display.

Hello! Hello!
Is what they shout
As through the traffic
We weave in and out.

Hello! Hello!
They wave and smile
As we pedal through
The city mile after mile.

Hello! Hello!
They shout and shriek
Breaking the monotony of
Each long week.

Hello! Hello!
They shout again
Hello, Hello has
Become our name!

ROBBIE WILLIAMS

This poem is best read rap-style, with a bit of youthful attitude! Unfortunately in this world there are teachers and others who, instead of encouraging young people, almost seem to take pleasure in knocking their confidence and dreams.

I, like the pop star Robbie Williams, felt little encouragement from certain teachers. Although I am not famous like Robbie, I had a dream beyond other people's perceptions of my abilities. The hidden track at the end of Robbie Williams' album *The Ego Has Landed* prompted me to write this poem. I believe we should give young people encouragement. Even if they are street children, they have a right to dream, and who knows? They may even be the next Robbie Williams. It's not for us to know, only for us to encourage and enjoy watching them surprise us – just like this young girl, whose life started on the streets. Because others believed in her, she now has a bright future and is studying at university.

Robbie Williams

I was a boy with an average education
But I had dreams beyond my situation.
The teachers said to me 'You won't go very far'
But look at Robbie Williams, he became a star!

My teenage life I had no clear direction
Then at nineteen I made a real connection
Changed my life, moved on from the past
My life before was nought but a farce.

The journey I started has led me to today;
Working with street children who don't have any say.
I've met many people who want to keep them down –
But a child has the right to be helped up from the ground.

They have low self-esteem and no expectations.
We raise their confidence so they have aspirations.
The future is for them if only others could perceive –
Allow them to dream and like Robbie they'll achieve.

A LIFE WITHOUT WORDS

Gair came into the street home after being brought up by her mother; they had lived together on the streets. Her mother had severe mental illness and had fallen into a fire, burning herself badly on the face, hands and body. She did not speak and Gair had spent her life mimicking her mother's noises to communicate with her. When first we met, she would use pointing, grunting and body and facial expressions to try to communicate. Chris and I spent a lot of time teaching her pencil skills and co-ordination (she could not even catch a ball when we first met her), while the house mother tried to teach her words, sounds and the alphabet. It was painful to watch as the penny slowly dropped that she was different from all the other children, particularly those of her age. She became closer to the very young children where language skills were not so important. Eventually an uncle was traced and, although very poor himself, he offered to take Gair and her mother to live with his family. On our last visit to see them, we took food and bought Gair some warm clothes for the coming winter. She is learning farming with her uncle and now speaks a little, but is still self-conscious, hiding her embarrassment behind her beautiful smile.

A Life Without Words

She was twelve years old, really quite sweet,
A great big smile and a dimpled cheek!
Arriving one night, ragged, alone,
After living on the streets she now had a home.
Given a nickname, they called her Gair.
This the new girl with the long dark hair.

A mother, insane, they'd lived in the gutter;
Gair mimicked her mother no words did she utter.
At first we all thought she was pulling a stunt
As she gestured and pointed, made sounds like a grunt.
She'd come from the streets, her story the same,
But she was different, let me explain –

This was a girl who was really quite unique,
At twelve years old, never learned to speak.
It's hard to imagine a life without words,
No adjectives, nouns, conjunctions or verbs.
It was painful to watch the realisation –
She needed words for communication.

THE GIFTS

Chris and I had been taking shoes, blankets and warm clothing around the villages to poor children. Tu said she had heard of a teenage street child who had just given birth. She had been taken in by a Christian community up in the mountains. The baby was eighteen days old, but as the young mother was malnourished herself, she was unable to produce any milk. We climbed high into the mountains to help, and were confronted by an almost biblical scene: An unmarried mother, a young baby, very basic shelter of tarpaulin with straw strewn across the muddy floor, and we three visitors bringing assistance. When we left a month later, the baby was doing much better.

The Gifts

High on a hill well out of view
Two aid workers with a guide named Tu.
The conditions wet, the scenery wild
Like the three wise men looking for a child.

Two thousand years on, we didn't follow a star,
The love of God brought us from afar
To an unmarried mother who had nowhere to go
And a Christian community, where compassion they show.

Living in poverty they still took her in
When everyone else just condemned her sin.
Made her a home with a straw-covered floor,
It was just like a stable without a door.

In this modern world, this ancient scene!
I pinched myself. It was not a dream!
A swaddling-clothed baby only eighteen days old
It was wet, it was muddy. It was bitterly cold.

The freezing air in this desolate place,
The child we held had death on its face.
No milk, the mother's own had gone dry.
Starving to death, this baby would die.

The wise men, they brought frankincense, myrrh and gold,
We gave milk, a bottle and a blanket for the cold.
The wise men they bowed down and worshipped a king,
We prayed for this baby whose life hung by a string.

RENT LABOUR FOR HIRE

When there is no welfare state, you have to find a way of earning your daily bread. When there is an oversupply of labour, what you get is the hardest work for the poorest pay. You never know from one day to the next if you will find someone to hire you, but you know if they don't, your family will go hungry.

Rent Labour for Hire

Rent labourers for hire! There are hungry mouths to feed.
Wages paid are really poor but satisfy the rich man's greed!
They get up really early with no guarantee of pay,
There won't be any money if they don't get hired that day.

Rent labourers for hire! Begging for some work.
The hunger in their stomachs makes it really hurt.
Whatever the weather they never get a break,
Surviving on the poorest diet, pushing heavy weights.

Rent labourers for hire! No time for being ill.
So many orphaned children, their fathers it has killed.
Although they work the hardest, they get paid the least.
The poor man gets the crumbs, the rich man eats the feast.

Rent labourers for hire! Capitalism at its worse.
An over supply of labour swells the rich man's purse.
The rich men getting richer with the masses staying poor.
Just one escape from poverty, and that is death for sure.

SUNSET ORPHAN

When Tam's father died, had if not been possible for her to come into a street children's home, she would have been left to live on the streets. When I first met her, she was still very sad over the loss of her father. Every night she would go to the front gate and stand transfixed, watching the sun as it set. Whilst I was working there she used to grab my arm and take me to watch this with her. I came to understand that while her father had been alive, it was their nightly ritual to watch the sunset together. As we stood there each night it brought back precious memories for her.

Sunset Orphan

Tam, a young orphan girl, her face so sad
Still mourning the passing of her dear dad.
Each night together they'd watch the sun set
Now she stands alone, but she won't forget.
His memory lives on in the bright red sky,
As the sun disappears, there's a tear in her eye.
Although he can't hug her, she still feels him there.
Unlike a street child, she had someone who cared.

THERE'S NEVER ENOUGH!

The challenge with poverty is that the scale of the problem is so great. Often we can go to give aid and, as soon as word gets around, double the amount of people arrive, far more than planned for or expected. This can be the most devastating emotion that one has to deal with. We never want anyone to be left out and refused the bare necessities of survival. We were able to give this boy a fleece to keep him warm, but there were no more shoes!

There's Never Enough!

Two children before you, both with no shoes.
Just one pair left, which one do you choose?
Five hundred pairs have been given before;
The challenge with poverty – there's always one more.

The choices you make can relieve someone's strife
Yet still leave another in the gutter of life.
When the money runs out and you've no more to give
With the last sack of food, then you choose who lives.
Confronted with this, which one would you choose?
Whatever your choice you know someone will lose.

THE RAT

It was one of the first times I had eaten at this particular street children's home. At the end of the meal, I offered to help clear up. That was when I was confronted by the big rat in the darkness.

Rats are an endemic problem – there is never a day when I don't see them running around the streets where I work. I have learnt to accept them, but try to avoid their company where possible. The picture above shows a couple of the children washing up during the day. In the background is the fencing through which the big rat waddles at night!

The Rat

Washing up dishes after the evening meal
Laughing and joking, it was so surreal!
Me and the street girls clanking the pot,
It was dark, it was humid. The evening was hot.

When out of the kitchen I saw it waddle
A fat rat the size of a Jack Russell!
I jumped up pointing with a bit of a start
As the rat waddled past and out into the dark.

The girls just looked on like 'What's all the fuss?
It's just another rat. Loads eat with us.'
The thing with Vietnam, there's rats everywhere
And when you're hungry it's another meal to share.

I think differently now, pretend it's a pet
As for sharing our meals, I try to forget.
The fat rat still waddles in every night
But I'm not washing up, I'm well out of sight!

SAFE AT NIGHT

At the end of a busy day at the street children's homes, it is nice to sit and enjoy the peace of the warm tropical evening. The silence is only broken by the nightly chorus of crickets clicking, and the children's laughter as they play games to unwind after a day at school. The beautiful, peaceful ambience is in complete contrast to what is happening just a short cycle ride away on the streets of the city, where these children once struggled to survive . . . the constant noise of motorcycles, the blaring music from the clubs and bars, the neon lights – and people, lots of people. This is what attracts street children to these areas to beg, sell gum, to shine shoes. Often it leaves them open to exploitation and danger.

In the warm evening breeze it is so special when I hear the children giggling in the darkness, talking, eating or just sitting quietly on their own; because I know that here they are safe at night.

Safe at Night

Clicking crickets, the warm evening breeze,
Leaves gently rustling on the swaying trees,
Diamonds twinkling from the black velvet sky;
All supervised by the moon's watchful eye.
Children's laughter echoes out in the dark.
A wonderful sound bringing warmth to my heart.
Each night the darkness has a beautiful charm,
The clicking of crickets, children free from harm.

TORN BETWEEN TWO WORLDS

It is the diversity of the two cultures I inhabit that prompted this poem. When I'm in England, I have a comfortable Western life: nice home, car and good lifestyle. When I'm working with street children, I have a small basic room, a 'sit up and beg' bicycle and I often eat where there are rats running around. I can lose as much as a stone in weight in a relatively short time.

Over the years I have been doing this work, there have been days when I yearned for the comforts of home. On these occasions, I have felt torn between the two worlds in which I move. But the truth is, when I am back in England, I yearn even more to get back to the children I work with. To my faithful pushbike and the squatty little room that is home.

Torn Between Two Worlds

The world from which I come is comfortable and secure;
No food and material needs, who could ever ask for more?
There's free health and education, no one has to pay;
Children have a childhood and leisure time to play.

But my eyes have been opened, another world I've seen
Where families live on pavements with no water to keep clean.
In day to day existence, they struggle to survive.
The picture's disturbing as it downloads before my eyes.

In the world from which I come, every life is valued,
But here amongst this poverty, there's a different attitude.
When I look around me, all I see is need;
Although our world seems perfect, are we blinkered by our greed?

Occasionally it hits me! I yearn the comforts of my home.
But when I'm back in England I think of all I have been shown.
As I stand here in this world, with its poverty unmasked,
I'm torn between two worlds, my future and my past.

SAY A PRAYER . . .

It's difficult for us in the West to imagine children as young as six years old living and sleeping on the streets, fending for themselves. Chris and I have met, seen and worked with many of these children and the poem is really just contrasting our secure life in England, where parents tuck their children into bed at night, with the reality in many developing and Third World countries.

Somewhere in the world, at this moment, a child is starting their journey of the street. Pray their journey is a safe one.

Say a Prayer . . .

If you are a parent, imagine your child,
Six years old, on the streets living wild.
Out in the darkness the whole of the night.
Drugs, prostitution, their future's not bright.
In parts of the world children live in this way.
They fight for survival day after day.
So tonight, when you tuck up your child in bed,
Say a prayer for the little ones, on the streets, unfed.